MATTER
CHANGING STATES

TARA HAELLE

rourkeeducationalmedia.com

Before & After Reading Activities

Teaching Focus:

Have students locate the ending punctuation for sentences in the book. Count how many times a period, question mark, or exclamation point is used. Which one is used the most? What is the purpose for each ending punctuation mark? Practice reading these sentences with appropriate expression.

Before Reading:

Building Academic Vocabulary and Background Knowledge

Before reading a book, it is important to set the stage for your child or student by using pre-reading strategies. This will help them develop their vocabulary, increase their reading comprehension, and make connections across the curriculum.

1. Look at the cover of the book. What will this book be about?
2. What do you already know about the topic?
3. Let's study the Table of Contents. What will you learn about in the book's chapters?
4. What would you like to learn about this topic? Do you think you might learn about it from this book? Why or why not?
5. Use a reading journal to write about your knowledge of this topic. Record what you already know about the topic and what you hope to learn about the topic.
6. Read the book.
7. In your reading journal, record what you learned about the topic and your response to the book.
8. After reading the book complete the activities below.

Content Area Vocabulary

Read the list. What do these words mean?

atoms
bond
chemical
element
energy
gravity
mass
molecule
volume
weight

After Reading:

Comprehension and Extension Activity

After reading the book, work on the following questions with your child or students to check their level of reading comprehension and content mastery.

1. What are the different ways matter can change states? *(Summarize)*
2. Why do people weigh less on Mars than on Earth? *(Infer)*
3. What happens if metal gets extremely hot? *(Asking Questions)*
4. When have you done something that caused a chemical change? *(Text to Self Connection)*
5. How does temperature affect matter? *(Asking Questions)*

Extension Activity

Design an experiment to test the boiling point of different liquids with an adult's help. Try adding substances such as sugar or salt to water to see if it changes the boiling point of the water. What do you think explains the results?

Table of Contents

Atoms Build Our World

Look around you. Take a deep breath. Listen closely. Everything you see, smell, hear, taste, and touch is matter. Matter makes up the universe, from the tiniest speck of dust to the largest stars in space.

Naming the Atom

A man named Democritus in Ancient Greece named the atom. *A* means *not*, and *tomos* means *cut* in Greek. Atoms are the smallest things that cannot be cut or destroyed.

All matter is made up of **atoms**. Atoms function like tiny building blocks. They are so small you cannot see them with just your eyes. It would take five million of the smallest atoms to cover the tip of a needle.

Atoms fit together like Legos to create larger pieces of matter. Even Legos are made of atoms! But atoms are not shaped like rectangles. They actually look like tiny solar systems.

Instead of a sun, atoms have a nucleus in the middle. The nucleus contains neutrons and protons, two types of particles. Particles are the tiniest pieces of matter we can count. Particles called electrons rotate rapidly around the nucleus just as planets revolve around the sun.

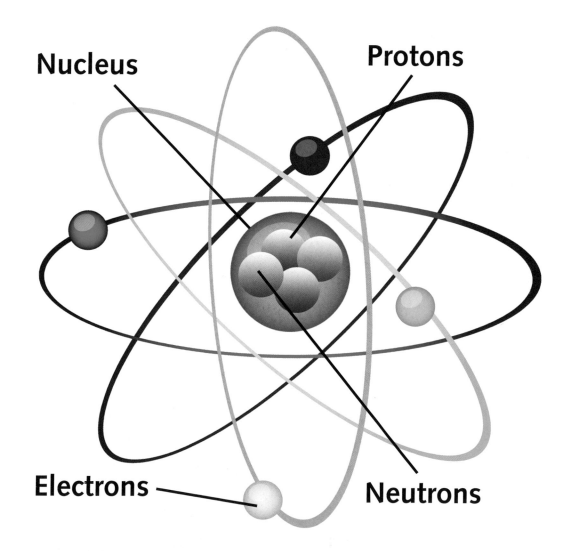

There are 118 different kinds of atoms. Each kind is called an **element.** The number of protons in the nucleus determines which element an atom is. The smallest element, hydrogen, has only one proton. Another element, helium, has two protons. Oxygen has eight protons.

Helium

Seeing Atoms
Scientists use a special microscope called an electron microscope to see atoms. They use beams of electrons instead of beams of light.

Let's Get Physical

Red

Green

Round

Physical Properties

When scientists study matter, they often describe its physical properties. Physical properties are characteristics you can observe without changing matter. For example, an apple's color and shape are two physical properties.

Another physical property is **mass**, or how much matter something contains. People use units, such as grams and kilograms, to describe mass. A tool called a balance measures mass by comparing one object to another.

The Perfect Kilogram

All kilograms are based on one special "perfect" kilogram stored in a vault in Paris. The kilogram is part of the metric system, which is used for measuring all sorts of physical properties.

An apple has an average mass of 3.53 ounces (100 grams). A raisin has a mass of about .035 ounces (1 gram). If you put an apple on one side of a balance, you would need about 100 raisins to make both sides of the balance equal.

Volume is another physical property. Volume describes how much space mass takes up. When you sit in a bathtub, the water rises because your volume takes up space. Your volume pushes the water up from where it was.

Effect of Gravity

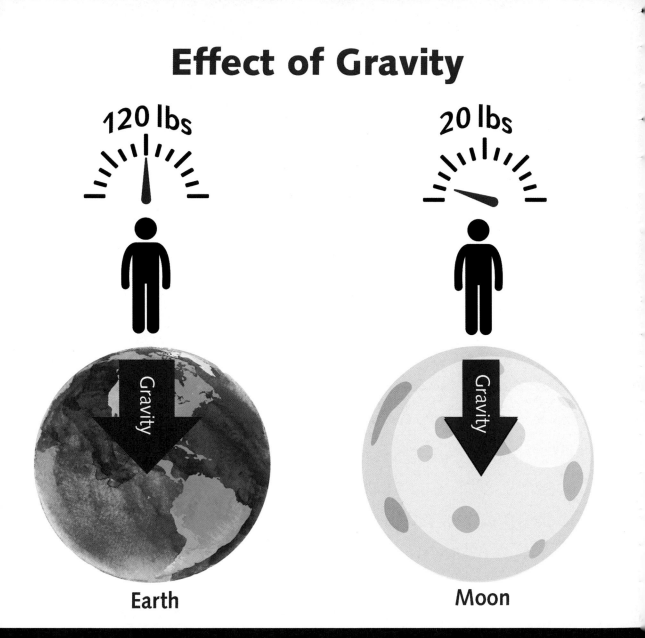

120 lbs

20 lbs

Gravity

Gravity

Earth

Moon

Weight is a physical property that describes the force of **gravity** pulling on an object. A scale measures weight. On Earth, the weight of an object is almost the same as its mass.

Away from Earth, though, weight changes when a place's gravitational pull is different. Jupiter has a much stronger gravitational pull than Earth because it's a much larger planet. The same object would weigh much more on Jupiter than on Earth.

Gravity Comparison Chart for a Person Weighing 100 Pounds (45 Kilograms)

Planet	Gravity Factor	Weight
Mercury	.38	38 lbs/17 kg
Venus	.90	90 lbs/41 kg
Earth	1.00	100 lbs/45 kg
Mars	.38	38 lbs/17 kg
Jupiter	2.60	260 lbs/118 kg
Saturn	1.07	107 lbs/49 kg
Uranus	1.17	117 lbs/53 kg
Neptune	1.22	122 lbs/55 kg

Moon Weight
How much would you weigh on the moon? The moon's gravity is 1/6th of Earth's gravity. So, divide your weight by six. That's your weight on the moon!

Different States of Matter

Atoms are constantly moving, but how much they can move around depends on their form. Matter exists in three common forms on Earth, as a solid, liquid, or gas. In solids, atoms are packed tightly together.

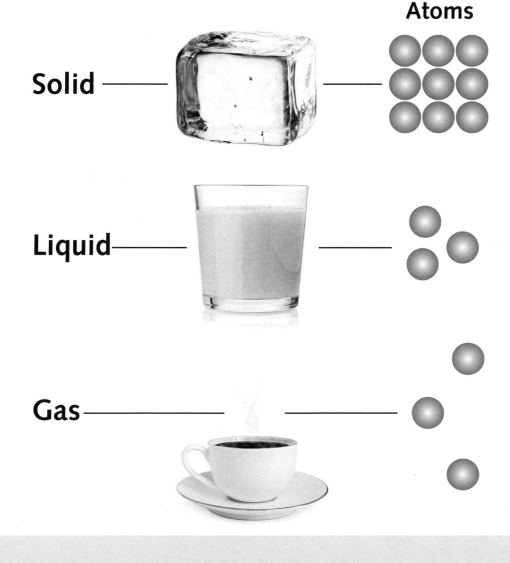

Atoms

Solid

Liquid

Gas

A solid has a definite shape, and its volume doesn't change. Most of what we see in our world are solids: buildings, metals, books, toys, clothing, and anything else that keeps its shape.

Fourth State
A fourth state, plasma, is rare on Earth but makes up 99 percent of our universe, including the sun. On Earth, plasma is found in lightning, electrical currents, and neon signs.

Atoms move around more freely in a liquid. The volume of liquids also doesn't change, but liquids take the shape of their container. Water in an Olympic swimming pool is rectangular, but water in a glass is the shape of a cylinder. Liquids can also flow or be poured.

In a gas, atoms are very spread out. Our air contains gases such as oxygen and nitrogen. Most gases are invisible, but they also take the shape of their container. The volume of a gas can also change. In a very small space, gas has less volume, but it expands to fill larger spaces.

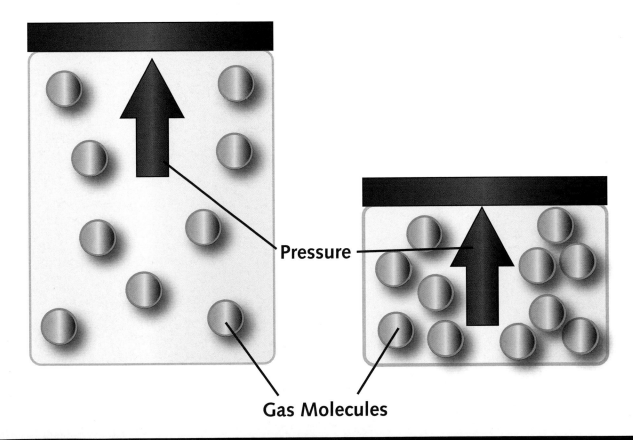

Pressure

Gas Molecules

Wondrous Water

Water is special because it's the only substance that exists naturally and abundantly on Earth in all three common states: solid as ice, liquid as water, and gas as water vapor.

How Matter Changes

Matter can physically change from one state to another by adding or removing heat. When water gets hot enough, it turns into water vapor. The process of changing from a liquid into a gas is called evaporation. Boiling water is evaporation in action. A towel dries as water slowly evaporates from it.

The temperature needed to change a substance from a liquid to a gas is its boiling point. Water's boiling point is 212 degrees Fahrenheit (100 degrees Celsius). Different substances have different boiling points.

212°F

80	hydrargyrum
Hg	
5d¹⁰6s²	200,59

$5d^{10}6s^2$ · 200,59 · 80 hydrargyrum · Hg

Quicksilver
Mercury is an unusual type of metal because it is a liquid at room temperature, giving it the nickname "quicksilver." Most metals are solid at room temperature.

Removing heat from water vapor changes it back into a liquid through a process called condensation. For example, water droplets often appear on a glass filled with cold water. That happens because water vapor near the glass loses heat as the heat moves to the cold water. With less heat, the vapor condenses into liquid water and forms droplets.

When water loses even more heat, it freezes into solid ice. A substance's freezing point is the temperature needed to change from a liquid into a solid. Water freezes at 32 degrees Fahrenheit (0 degrees Celsius).

32°F

Solid to Gas

Another physical change is the process of sublimation, changing from a solid directly to a gas. Dry ice is solid carbon dioxide that converts immediately to gas at room temperature.

These physical changes are reversible because changing the temperature again can convert a substance back into its previous state. Ice melts into water again when heated.

Grow Your Own Crystals

When a solid mixes with a liquid, sometimes the solid dissolves and becomes part of the liquid. If the liquid evaporates, it leaves the solid behind. The solid sometimes forms crystals. You can watch this happen by growing your own crystals.

You will need:

dark colored construction paper
a baking pan large enough to lay the paper in
Epson salts
warm water
measuring cup
spoon
table salt
sugar
optional: food coloring

Instructions:

1. Lay the colored paper in the pan.
2. Mix 1 tablespoon (14.8 milliliters) of Epson salts with ¼ cup (59 milliliters) of warm water until the salts dissolve.
3. Pour the water and Epson salts mixture into the pan. Leave it in a flat, still place.
4. Check on the pan after one hour. What do you see happening?
5. Leave the pan and return after another hour. Keep returning each hour to see what happens.
6. Optional: Do the experiment again and add food coloring to the mixture first. Can you make different colored crystals?
7. Optional: Try the experiment again with different substances, such as table salt and sugar. What happens if you mix more or less of the substance in the water first?

Chemicals React!

Physical changes are reversible, but substances can also undergo **chemical** changes. Chemical changes are not reversible because they change the way a substance's atoms are arranged. It becomes a completely new substance.

Atoms can **bond** together into molecules. A **molecule** is any combination of at least two atoms. The oxygen we breathe is O_2, two oxygen molecules bonded together.

Remember that different kinds of atoms are called elements. A molecule with more than one element is a compound. Water is a compound because each molecule has two hydrogen atoms and one oxygen atom.

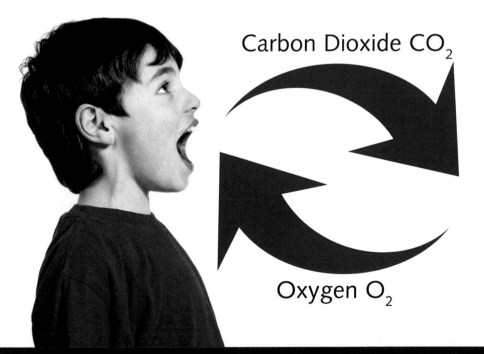

Carbon Dioxide CO_2

Oxygen O_2

Chemical vs. Physical Changes
Mixing sugar and water looks like a chemical change because the sugar seems to disappear. But it's actually a physical change. Add heat, and the water evaporates, leaving the sugar behind.

Chemical changes require adding or removing **energy.** During a chemical change of water, energy breaks apart the molecule's bonds. The hydrogen and oxygen atoms separate and become available to make a new substance.

The process of a chemical change is called a chemical reaction. Rust is a chemical change that happens when iron and oxygen react. Two iron atoms react with three oxygen atoms and create a new substance, rust.

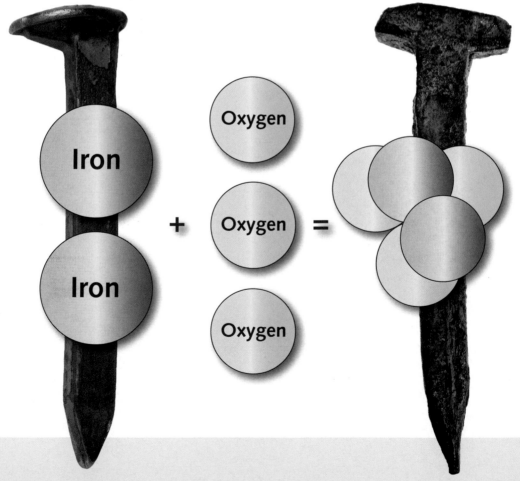

Make a Chemical Reaction!

Sometimes a chemical reaction is dangerous, such as exploding dynamite. But some chemical reactions are safe and fun to watch. You can see what happens when two chemicals react.

You will need:
baking soda
white vinegar
measuring cup
several glass jars or other containers
optional: food coloring
a cake pan and medicine dropper
dish soap or bubbles soap
optional: food coloring

Instructions:
1. Find an open space where you can do the experiment and clean up easily afterward. It could be a mess, so lay down plastic or do it outside.
2. Fill each container about halfway with vinegar.
3. Optional: Add different food colors to the different jars.
4. Add at least a quarter cup (59 milliliters) of baking soda to the vinegar mixture.
5. Watch what happens!
6. Optional: Try adding dish soap or bubbles mixture to the vinegar first. What happens when you add the baking soda?
7. Optional: Cover the bottom of the baking pan with baking soda. Add food coloring to some vinegar and add it to the medicine dropper. Use the medicine dropper to drop colorful vinegar onto the baking soda.

What happened when you added the baking soda? Vinegar is a type of chemical called an acid. Baking soda is a type of chemical called a base. When you mix an acid and base, it causes a chemical reaction. The new substance created was carbon dioxide.

27

Just as substances have physical properties, they have chemical properties too. Chemical properties can only be observed during or after a chemical reaction, such as changes in color or smell.

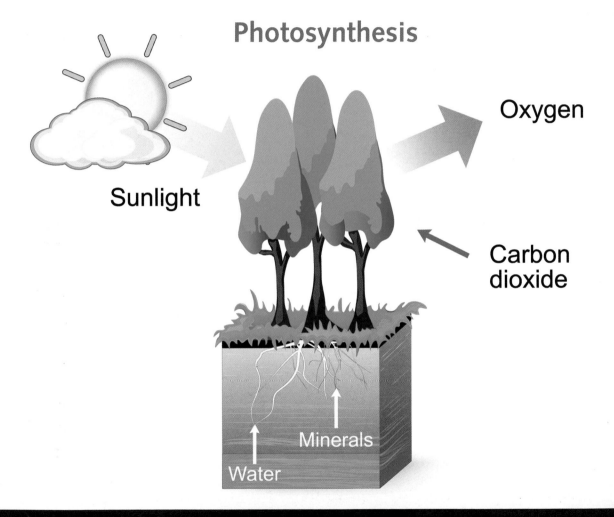

Photosynthesis

Sunlight

Oxygen

Carbon dioxide

Minerals

Water

Plant Power
Plants create chemical reactions all day long in order to eat. They convert the sun's energy and carbon dioxide into sugar and oxygen through a process called photosynthesis.

Cooking is an example of a chemical change. You cannot "uncook" a substance because its atoms have rearranged into a new substance. If you roast a marshmallow over a fire, it becomes a brown, gooey, yummy blob!

Glossary

atoms (AT-uhmz): the tiniest parts of an element that have all the properties of that element; all the matter in the universe is made up of atoms

bond (bahnd): when you bond two things, you make them stick together

chemical (KEM-i-kuhl): a substance used in or made by chemistry, as in household chemicals

element (EL-uh-muhnt): a substance that cannot be divided up into simpler substances

energy (EN-ur-jee): the ability of something to do work; energy is a concept in physics and is measured in joules

gravity (GRAV-i-tee): the force that pulls things toward the center of Earth or other physical body having mass and keeps them from floating away

mass (mas): the amount of physical matter that an object contains

molecule (MAH-luh-kyool): the smallest unit that a chemical compound can be divided into that still displays all of its chemical properties. A molecule is made up of more than one atom.

volume (VAHL-yuhm): the amount of space taken up by a three-dimensional object, such as a box, or by a substance within a container

weight (wate): a measurement that shows how heavy someone or something is

Index

Show What You Know

1. What are the three particles that make up an atom?

2. What physical property changes depending on how strong gravity is?

3. What are the three common states of matter?

4. What is the process of turning from a liquid into a gas called?

5. What is needed to cause a chemical change?

Websites to Visit

www.learninggamesforkids.com/
   changes-in-matter-games.html

www.chem4kids.com/files/react_intro.html

www.exploratorium.edu/ronh/weight

About the Author

Tara Haelle spent much of her youth exploring creeks and forests outside and reading books inside. Her adventures became bigger when she became an adult and began traveling across the world on exciting adventures such as swimming with sharks, climbing Mt. Kilimanjaro, exploring the Amazon, and eating insects! She earned a master's degree in photojournalism from the University of Texas at Austin so she could keep learning about the world by talking to scientists and writing about their work. She currently lives in central Illinois with her husband, two sons, two Chihuahuas, and two cats. You can learn more about her at www.tarahaelle.net.

Meet The Author!
www.meetREMauthors.com

www.rourkeeducationalmedia.com

PHOTO CREDITS: Cover and title page: ©filipfoto; table of contents: ©zaklad; p.4-5, 29: ©Nick_Pandevonium; p.5: ©pmcdonald; p.6: ©johavel; p.7: ©generalfmv, ©MicroStockHub, ©Rich Legg; p.8: ©hdere; p.9: ©xefstock, ©2007 AFP; p.11: ©Dennis Moskvinov, ©Jag_cz; p.14: ©ryasick, ©Evgeny Karandaev, ©Ninell_Art; p.15: ©Justin Horrocks, ©photocritical; p.16: ©ConstantinosZ, ©abadonian; p.18: ©suriya silsaksom; p.19: ©Magnascan, ©AlexLMX; p.20: ©ALEAIMAGE, ©Florea Marius Catalin; p.21: ©Liz Leyden, ©paylessimages; p.22: ©mikdam; p.23: ©Coprid; p.24: ©summertree1914; p.25: ©zveiger alexandre; p.26: ©&#169 bonnie jacobs, ©roibu; p.29: ©MCCAIG

Edited by: Keli Sipperley
Cover design by: Rhea Magaro-Wallace
Interior design by: Kathy Walsh

Library of Congress PCN Data

Matter Changing States / Tara Haelle
 (Science Alliance)
  ISBN 978-1-68342-345-4 (hard cover)
  ISBN 978-1-68342-441-3 (soft cover)
  ISBN 978-1-68342-511-3 (e-Book)
Library of Congress Control Number: 2017931189

Rourke Educational Media
Printed in the United States of America, North Mankato, Minnesota